Born to the
VIRGIN
MARY

Born to the
VIRGIN
MARY

DAVID J. RIDGES

CFI
An Imprint of Cedar Fort, Inc.
Springville, Utah

The cover art of this book was created by Annie Henrie and is entitled "Love's Pure Light."

This is not an official publication of The Church of Jesus Christ of Latter-day Saints. The opinions and views expressed herein belong solely to the author and do not necessarily represent the opinions or views of Cedar Fort, Inc. Permission for the use of sources, graphics, and photos is also solely the responsibility of the author.

ISBN 13: 978-1-4621-1512-9

Published by CFI, an imprint of Cedar Fort, Inc.
2373 W. 700 S., Springville, UT 84663
Distributed by Cedar Fort, Inc., www.cedarfort.com

LIBRARY OF CONGRESS CATALOGING-IN-PUBLICATION DATA

Ridges, David J., author.
Born to the Virgin Mary / David J. Ridges.
    pages cm
Summary: Uses scriptures to tell of the Savior's birth and early life.
ISBN 978-1-4621-1512-9 (alk. paper)
1. Jesus Christ--Nativity. 2. Jesus Christ--Mormon interpretations. 3. Church of Jesus Christ of Latter-day Saints--Doctrines. I. Title.

BX8643.J4R525 2014
232.92--dc23

                                    2014021310

Cover design by Shawnda T. Craig
Cover design © 2014 Lyle Mortimer
Edited and typeset by Kevin Haws

Printed in the United States of America

10 9 8 7 6 5 4 3 2 1

Printed on acid-free paper

Dedication

To my wife, Janette, whose love, friendship,
and support are priceless.

Mother and Son

Think, if you will, of the close relationship and deep feelings of love between the Savior and His mortal mother, Mary. Imagine the bond between mother and Son that grew deep as eternity during their brief mortality together. Consider how it must be even now, having both entered into eternity where their sacred family ties last forever. Think of the satisfaction they both had, serving together, each fulfilling their assigned divine mission—the miraculous virgin birth through Mary and the miracle of the atoning sacrifice provided by the Savior, bringing immortality and the potential for exaltation to all.

Mary is universally held in highest esteem among believers. Her name, "Mary," is one of the most popular given names for baby girls throughout the Christian world. She is reverenced and revered for her beauty of soul and humble acceptance of the angel's Annunciation to her that she was the chosen, pure vessel who was to fulfill the ancient prophecy of the Messiah's virgin birth. She is depicted in paintings, drawings, poetry, literature, and sculpture as an example of tranquil steadfastness in tenderly nurturing and teaching the infant Savior of the world.

During the final scenes of the Crucifixion, as her Son hung in agony on the cruel cross, we sense her own agony as she looked on. Tenderly, her beloved Son called to John, instructing him to take care of His mother after He was gone (John 19:26–27). She knew who He was and that this hour had to come, but no doubt the terrible reality of it was far more than she could have anticipated. We have no doubt that the Holy Ghost strengthened her for this unimaginable ordeal. We also feel her exquisite joy at His Resurrection, made all the sweeter because of having tasted the indescribable bitter.

While the scriptures are silent regarding her life from this point on, except for one brief statement in Acts 1:14, in which we are informed that she was with the Apostles after the Savior's Resurrection and Ascension, we trust that she would have seen her Son during the forty days of His ministry (Acts 1:3) before His Ascension to heaven. Imagine how tender the relationship must be now between Jesus and His mortal mother!

The Annunciation

In a vision, the prophet Abraham was shown "many of the noble and great ones" (Abraham 3:22) who would play significant roles in bringing salvation to the Father's spirit children as he sent us to earth. As we think about Mary, the mother of the Son of God, it seems likely that she was among these powerful and valiant spirits. We gain wonderful insight into her noble and great soul as we read her humble response to the Annunciation by the angel Gabriel (Noah—see Bible Dictionary under "Gabriel") that she was to be the mother of the promised Messiah. Her faith exemplifies her spiritual maturity and provides a window to her soul. Her response is brief and uncomplicated, typical of people of great faith.

> And Mary said, Behold the handmaid of the Lord; be it unto me according to thy word. (Luke 1:38)

As she visited Elizabeth, who was six months along with her own miracle, the coming birth of John the Baptist in her extreme old age, Mary gives us yet more evidence of her preeminent place among our premortal spirit brothers and sisters. After hearing Elizabeth prophesy (Luke 1:42–45), Mary herself is filled with the glorious spirit of prophecy. I will include brief commentary as well as contributions from the JST (Joseph Smith Translation of the Bible) as we read Mary's prophecy.

Luke 1:46–55
And Mary said, My soul doth magnify [*praise*] the Lord,
And my spirit hath rejoiced in God my Saviour.

JST Luke 1:46
And my spirit rejoiceth in God my Savior.

It is touching to realize that Mary's baby would be her Savior as well as her child. From the verses we are reading here, it seems clear that she was well versed in the scriptures and understood that these prophecies pertained to the child whom she would now bear.

For he hath regarded [*seen, considered*] the low estate [*humble condition*] of his handmaiden [*servant*]: for, behold, from henceforth all generations shall call me blessed [*from now on, all people will know me and know how blessed I am*].

For he that is mighty [*God*] hath done to me great things; and holy is his name.

JST Luke 1:48
For he who is mighty hath done to me great things; and I will magnify his holy name,

And his mercy is on them that fear [*respect and obey*] him from generation to generation.

In verses 51–55, we gain further insights into the depth of Mary's understanding concerning the coming Messiah.

He hath shewed [*demonstrated*] strength with his arm [*has shown His power*]; he hath scattered [*punished*] the proud in the imagination of their hearts [*because of their pride*].

He hath put down [*humbled*] the mighty from their seats [*positions of power*], and exalted them of low degree [*blessed and lifted up the humble*].

He hath filled the hungry [*those who "hunger and thirst after righteousness"; see Matthew 5:6*] with good things; and the rich [*the rich who are prideful*] he hath sent empty away.

He hath holpen [*helped*] his servant Israel [*the covenant people*], in remembrance of his mercy;

As he spake to our fathers [*ancestors*], to Abraham, and to his seed [*posterity*] for ever.

Though elsewhere in the scriptures we find relatively little about Mary, the above verses give us deep insights into her strength and noble character as she now prepares to bring the Savior into this world for His thirty-three years as the Mortal Messiah.

Christ's Mortal Mission Draws Nigh

As the time for His mortal mission drew near, think how it must have been for the Savior. Finally, He, the Redeemer chosen in the grand premortal council, was to experience mortality for Himself. After creating "worlds without number" (Moses 1:33) for the Father, now He would actually be born on this one. Think how He must have felt, several years before His own birth, as Joseph's time came to leave the premortal spirit life and come to earth to be born. Was there a tender farewell scene where Jesus embraced Joseph, as they contemplated their future lives on earth together? Did Jesus express special gratitude for this humble and noble man who would be His wonderful stepfather, who would protect Him and His mother, who would teach Him the carpenter's trade, and who would provide a righteous home for Him and His mother, along with His half-brothers and sisters?

What was it like when it came time for Mary to leave our premortal heavenly home and enter the body that her own mortal mother was preparing for her? Did Mary and Jesus embrace and whisper, "I love you" to each other as she departed? What thoughts were going through the Savior's mind, knowing that in just a few short years, He too would have the veil of forgetfulness drawn over His supreme mind and enter a state of helplessness and dependency upon Mary and Joseph?

We know from the scriptures that Jesus did have the veil drawn over His mind as He came forth as a newborn infant. He "grew, and waxed strong in spirit . . . and . . . increased in wisdom" (Luke 2:40, 52). Elder James E. Talmage explained this as follows:

> He came among men to experience all the natural conditions of mortality; He was born as truly a dependent, helpless babe as is any other child; His infancy was in all common features as the infancy of others; His boyhood was actual boyhood, His development was as necessary and as real as that of all children. Over His mind had fallen the veil of forgetfulness common to all who are born to earth, by which the remembrance of primeval existence is shut off. The Child grew, and with growth there came to Him expansion of mind, development of faculties, and progression in power and understanding. (*Jesus the Christ*, 111)

To Be Born in Bethlehem

The Old Testament prophet Micah had prophesied more than seven hundred years before the Savior's birth that Bethlehem, a small village of no particular importance commercially, would be the birthplace of the Messiah.

But thou, Beth-lehem Ephratah, though thou be little among the thousands of Judah, yet out of thee shall He [the Savior] come forth unto me that is to be ruler in Israel; whose goings forth have been from of old, from everlasting. (Micah 5:2)

This prophecy that the Messiah was to be born in the obscure village of Bethlehem seems to have been well known at the time of the birth of Christ. In fact, when the Wise Men approached King Herod to ask where the "King of the Jews" (Matthew 2:2) had been born, the king's advisers had no trouble coming up with the answer that it was prophesied to be Bethlehem, which was about five miles south of Jerusalem.

And when he had gathered all the chief priests and scribes of the people together, he demanded of them where Christ should be born.

And they said unto him, In Bethlehem of Judæa: for thus it is written by the prophet,

And thou Bethlehem, in the land of Juda, art not the least among the princes of Juda: for out of thee shall come a Governor, that shall rule my people Israel. (Matthew 2:4–6)

The Journey from Nazareth to Bethlehem

As the time for the Savior's mortal birth drew near, Joseph and Mary were living in Nazareth, a village about sixty miles straight north of Bethlehem, but actually around 130–40 miles from Bethlehem based on the common travel routes, avoiding Samaria, which Jews would likely take to go from Galilee into Judea. Nazareth was a town in the hill country of Galilee, and we suppose that it was there that Joseph received word of Caesar's decree that all his subjects were to register for taxation. At that time, the Holy Land was part of the vast Mediterranean area ruled by Rome under Caesar

Augustus (he ruled the Roman Empire for forty-five years, from 31 BC to AD 14). Luke sets the stage for the difficult journey Joseph and Mary had from Galilee to Bethlehem.

> And it came to pass in those days, that there went out a decree from Cæsar Augustus, that all the world should be taxed.
>
> (And this taxing was first made when Cyrenius was governor of Syria.)
>
> And all went to be taxed, every one into his own city.
>
> And Joseph also went up from Galilee, out of the city of Nazareth, into Judæa, unto the city of David, which is called Bethlehem; (because he was of the house and lineage of David:)
>
> To be taxed with Mary his espoused wife, being great with child. (Luke 2:1–5)

James E. Talmage explains that, normally, Joseph could have registered right in Nazareth, but because of Jewish custom, he went to register in Bethlehem.

> At that time a decree went out from Rome ordering a taxing of the people in all kingdoms and provinces tributary to the empire; the call was of general scope, it provided "that all the world should be taxed." The taxing herein referred to may properly be understood as an enrolment, or a registration, whereby a census of Roman subjects would be secured, upon which as a basis the taxation of the different peoples would be determined. This particular census was the second of three such general registrations recorded by historians as occurring at intervals of about twenty years. Had the census been taken by the usual Roman method, each person would have been enrolled at the town of his residence; but the Jewish custom, for which the Roman law had respect, necessitated registration at the cities or towns claimed by the respective families as their ancestral homes. As to whether the requirement was strictly mandatory that every family should thus register at the city of its ancestors, we need not be specially

concerned; certain it is that Joseph and Mary went to Bethlehem, the city of David, to be inscribed under the imperial decree. (*Jesus the Christ*, 91–92)

Thus Joseph and Mary traveled to Bethlehem, the prophesied place of the Savior's birth. It may well be that, as they approached the village, Mary was already experiencing labor pains. If so, it would have been extra difficult for her and would have caused Joseph much additional worry and concern for the well-being of his young wife. Before we continue with Joseph and Mary as they arrive in Bethlehem, we will go half a world away and listen in as Nephi is told that this is the night of the Savior's birth.

The Voice of the Lord Tells Nephi the Time for His Birth Has Come

Remember that the enemies of the Church among the wicked Nephites in America had set a deadline for the fulfillment of the promised sign of the Savior's birth. There was to be a "day and a night and a day, as if it were one day," as foretold by Samuel the Lamanite about five years previous (Helaman 14:4). This would serve as unmistakable evidence that the Christ child had been born. If the sign did not come by the deadline, they would execute the believers. It had not yet come and the deadline was about up. The wicked were preparing for the imminent slaughter of the hated faithful believers in Christ. As Nephi bowed in sorrow and worry for his people in fervent prayer, the voice of the Lord came to him with the joyous news.

> Lift up your head and be of good cheer; for behold, the time
> is at hand, and on this night shall the sign be given, and on
> the morrow come I into the world, to show unto the world
> that I will fulfil all that which I have caused to be spoken by
> the mouth of my holy prophets.

Behold, I come unto my own, to fulfil all things which I have made known unto the children of men from the foundation of the world, and to do the will, both of the Father and of the Son—of the Father because of me, and of the Son because of my flesh. And behold, the time is at hand, and this night shall the sign be given. (3 Nephi 1:13–14)

Sure enough, as the sun went down, the sky did not get dark. The sign was given and the prophecy was fulfilled. Imagine the joy of Nephi and the relief among the Nephite believers as their faithfulness against all odds was rewarded. Picture also the terror and confusion among the unbelievers as they faced the startling fact that they were wrong and wicked. Gratefully, many of these were converted and baptized (1 Nephi 1:22–23). Thus, the Atonement worked for them, cleansing and healing them and giving them a fresh start.

The fact that this message was given to Nephi from the Savior the day before His birth leads us to suppose that it was likely given while Mary was in labor. Students of this part of the Book of Mormon often marvel at what a miracle it was that Jesus' spirit left His tiny body in Mary's womb to give this message to Nephi. However, we need to be a bit careful with this. While such a miracle is certainly possible with God, 3 Nephi 1:12 says that it was "the voice of the Lord." With this in mind, we realize that there are perhaps several possibilities. The Lord could have left His body to be near Nephi and spoken to him that way. The Savior also could have spoken from Bethlehem and used His power to have Nephi hear Him. Or the Holy Ghost, who can speak for the Son as if He were speaking (Moses 5:9), could have spoken to Nephi and delivered the Savior's message. Whatever the case, a marvelous manifestation was given to Nephi, and that night, when the sun went down, it remained as light as day, thus witnessing to the Nephites that the Son of God was to be born to Mary (Mosiah 3:8) the next day in the city of Bethlehem. We will now return to Joseph and Mary.

No Room at the Inn

As a worried Joseph and a weary Mary arrived in Bethlehem, it must have been a relief to finally be at the end of the journey. But it is likely that this relief quickly changed to deep discouragement as Joseph's pleading inquiries for a room to stay in were repeatedly turned down. Throngs of people crowded the streets and the inns were full. It is interesting to note that the Bible, as it stands, mentions just one "inn" (Luke 2:7). However, the JST's use of the word "inns" (JST, Luke 2:7; see Luke 2:7, footnote b in the English version of the LDS edition of the King James Bible) indicates that Joseph enquired at several inns. Finally, arrangements were made for the most humble of accommodations in a stable, likely surrounded by domestic animals, with a manger that could serve as a bed for the newborn child. Perhaps you've noticed that the Bible gives very little detail about this scene. Thus, most everything we hear and see about it is based on tender and worshipful opinion and imagination of authors, artists, playwrights, filmmakers, and others, as to how things actually were. The eternally important matter is that the Son of God had now been born.

> And so it was, that, while they were there, the days were accomplished that she should be delivered.
>
> And she brought forth her firstborn son, and wrapped him in swaddling clothes, and laid him in a manger; because there was no room for them in the inn. (Luke 2:6–7)

Just a note about swaddling clothes. They were bands of cloth in which a newborn baby was wrapped. The baby was placed diagonally upon a square piece of cloth. The bottom corner of the square cloth was folded up to cover the baby's feet and the side corners were then folded in to cover the baby's sides. Then bands of cloth were wound around the baby to make a warm, comfortable bundle.

Shepherds See and Then Bear Witness

Even though we celebrate Christmas on December 25, along with the majority of the modern Christian world, we understand that it was actually springtime when the Savior was born. President Kimball taught that Christ was born on April 6.

> "The hinge of history is on the door of a Bethlehem stable." (Ralph Sockman.) The name Jesus Christ and what it represents has been plowed deep into the history of the world, never to be uprooted. Christ was born on the sixth of April. ("Why Call Me Lord, Lord, and Do Not the Things Which I Say?" par. 9)

In one of the revelations given at the time of the official organization of the Church, which was specified by the Savior to take place on April 6, 1830, we see an implication that April 6 is of personal significance to Him.

> The rise of the Church of Christ in these last days, being one thousand eight hundred and thirty years since the coming of our Lord and Savior Jesus Christ in the flesh, it being regularly organized and established agreeable to the laws of our country, by the will and commandments of God, in the fourth month, and on the sixth day of the month which is called April. (D&C 20:1)

Thus, shepherds in the Bethlehem area would have been grazing their sheep on the fresh new growth of spring and watching over them by night when the Christ child was born. Certain of these shepherds had the great privilege of having an angel announce the birth of Christ to them, telling them that they would find Him in a manger.

And there were in the same country shepherds abiding in the field, keeping watch over their flock by night.

And, lo, the angel of the Lord came upon them, and the glory of the Lord shone round about them: and they were sore afraid.

And the angel said unto them, Fear not: for, behold, I bring you good tidings of great joy, which shall be to all people.

For unto you is born this day in the city of David a Saviour, which is Christ the Lord.

And this shall be a sign unto you; Ye shall find the babe wrapped in swaddling clothes, lying in a manger. (Luke 2:8–12)

This angel was joined by a vast multitude of angels singing praises and rejoicing in the holy birth of the Savior.

And suddenly there was with the angel a multitude of the heavenly host praising God, and saying,

Glory to God in the highest, and on earth peace, good will toward men. (Luke 2:13–14)

When the shepherds recovered sufficiently from their initial fear and shock, they hurried to Bethlehem to see the newly born Son of God. And after having done so, they became witnesses to the glorious event and spread the word abroad.

And it came to pass, as the angels were gone away from them into heaven, the shepherds said one to another, Let us now go even unto Bethlehem, and see this thing which is come to pass, which the Lord hath made known unto us.

And they came with haste, and found Mary, and Joseph, and the babe lying in a manger.

And when they had seen it, they made known abroad the saying which was told them concerning this child. (Luke 2:15–17)

Mary Kept These Things in Her Heart

In spite of the fact that the shepherds had been told by angelic hosts that Mary's child was indeed the "Saviour, which is Christ the Lord" (Luke 2:11), and that they bore witness of their heavenly experience to many, we suppose that there must have been many things about this special child and His birth that Mary and Joseph could not share with those around them. To do so would have been premature and no doubt invited ridicule and scorn, and perhaps even persecution. They both knew personally, by way of heavenly messages given them by angels, that this was the promised Messiah, the Son of the Most High God, the Redeemer of the world, foretold in almost countless prophecies by ancient prophets of God. But to share or explain more about who the child really was would not have been wise. Luke summarizes this and much more in a simple phrase:

> But Mary kept all these things, and pondered them in her heart. (Luke 2:19)

Joseph and Mary Kept the Law of Moses

According to the law of Moses, all male children were to be circumcised when eight days old (Leviticus 12:3) as a token of the covenant that the Lord made with Abraham (Genesis 17:9–12). This was the practice during Old Testament dispensations and continued among the Jews at the time of the Savior's birth. The custom among the Jews was to also give the child a name at the time of circumcision (Bible Dictionary, "Circumcision"). Luke makes brief reference to these things as he gives his account of the Savior's earliest mortal days.

And when eight days were accomplished for the circumcising of the child, his name was called Jesus, which was so named of the angel before he was conceived in the womb. (Luke 2:21)

The law of circumcision was done away with as the Savior fulfilled the law of Moses during His mortal mission (Galatians 5:1–6). Thus it was no longer required in the New Testament church, after Jesus established it.

Simeon and Anna in the Temple

After waiting the forty days after the birth of a male child required by the law of Moses for purification (Leviticus 12:2–4), Mary and Joseph took the infant Jesus to the temple to dedicate Him to the Lord. Under the law of Moses, first-born males were to be dedicated to the Lord.

And the Lord spake unto Moses, saying,
Sanctify unto me all the firstborn, whatsoever openeth the womb among the children of Israel, both of man and of beast: it is mine. (Exodus 13:1–2)

Can you see the symbolism in this? It is another example of Atonement symbolism in the law of Moses. It represented, among other things, that the "Firstborn" of the Father would be dedicated to carry out the work of the Father through His mission and Atonement. So it was that Joseph and Mary, faithful to the laws of God in their day, took Jesus to the temple to dedicate Him to the Lord. They purchased the required sacrifices and proceeded.

And when the days of her purification according to the law of Moses were accomplished, they brought him to Jerusalem, to present him to the Lord;
(As it is written in the law of the Lord, Every male that openeth the womb shall be called holy to the Lord;)

> And to offer a sacrifice according to that which is said
> in the law of the Lord, A pair of turtledoves, or two young
> pigeons. (Luke 2:22–24)

While they were in the temple on this special occasion, a righteous man by the name of Simeon, who was apparently quite elderly, no doubt excitedly—but reverently—approached them and took the infant Jesus in his arms. Simeon had been promised through the Holy Ghost that he would not die until he had seen the promised Messiah in the flesh. With great joy and satisfaction now that the promised blessing had been realized, Simeon exclaimed that he could now die in peace.

> And, behold, there was a man in Jerusalem, whose name was
> Simeon; and the same man was just and devout, waiting for
> the consolation of Israel: and the Holy Ghost was upon him.
> And it was revealed unto him by the Holy Ghost, that
> he should not see death, before he had seen the Lord's Christ.
> And he came by the Spirit into the temple: and when
> the parents brought in the child Jesus, to do for him after
> the custom of the law,
> Then took he him up in his arms, and blessed God,
> and said,
> Lord, now lettest thou thy servant depart in peace,
> according to thy word:
> For mine eyes have seen thy salvation,
> Which thou hast prepared before the face of all people;
> A light to lighten the Gentiles, and the glory of thy
> people Israel. (Luke 2:25–32)

It is evident in what Luke says next that he understood well that Mary was the mother of Jesus, but Joseph was not His father. This is a brief but significant verse of scripture bearing witness that Jesus Christ was the Son of God. Luke did not say, "His father and mother," rather,

And Joseph and his mother marvelled at those things which were spoken of him. (Luke 2:33)

While the Spirit was upon Simeon, he continued, prophesying of the great mission of Mary's child and reminding us of the pain that she would yet go through as His mother.

And Simeon blessed them, and said unto Mary his mother, Behold, this child is set for the fall and rising again of many in Israel; and for a sign which shall be spoken against;

(Yea, a sword shall pierce through thy own soul also,) that the thoughts of many hearts may be revealed. (Luke 2:34–35)

The Joseph Smith Translation of the Bible makes changes to verse 35.

JST Luke 2:35

Yea, a spear shall pierce through *him to the wounding of thine own soul also*; that the thoughts of many hearts may be revealed.

Next, Luke tells us that an elderly woman, also in the temple at the same time, approached them just as Simeon was finishing his inspired utterances. She also witnessed to those present that this child was the Son of God. Her name was Anna, and she was from the tribe of Asher (one of the Twelve Tribes of Israel). Her husband had died seven years after they were married. If we understand Luke correctly, it appears that she was about eighty-four years old at this time.

And there was one Anna, a prophetess, the daughter of Phanuel, of the tribe of Aser: she was of a great age, and had lived with an husband seven years from her virginity;

And she was a widow of about fourscore and four years, which departed not from the temple, but served God with fastings and prayers night and day.

And she coming in that instant gave thanks likewise unto the Lord, and spake of him to all them that looked for redemption in Jerusalem. (Luke 2:36–38)

The Wise Men

The scriptures do not tell us how long after the birth of Jesus that the Wise Men visited Him and presented their gifts to Him. Suffice it to say that by the time of their visit, He is referred to as a "young child" (Matthew 2:11, 13) and Joseph and Mary along with the Christ child were living in a house somewhere in Bethlehem (Matthew 2:11). The scriptures are also silent as to the origins of the Wise Men, how many there were, their names, or much of anything about them. It will be interesting to learn more about these great men, perhaps at the time of the Second Coming, when "all things" will be revealed (D&C 101:32). In the meantime, we do know that they came from the East, that they had seen the new star, and that they were aware that it signaled the birth of the Son of God.

Now when Jesus was born in Bethlehem of Judæa in the days of Herod the king, behold, there came wise men from the east to Jerusalem,

Saying, Where is he that is born King of the Jews? for we have seen his star in the east, and are come to worship him. (Matthew 2:1–2)

The JST makes a significant change to verse 2, above. Notice what Joseph Smith substituted for "King of the Jews."

JST Matthew 2:2
Saying, *Where is the child that is born, the Messiah* of the Jews? for we have seen his star in the east, and have come to worship him.

King Herod was a cruel and hypocritical tyrant, much feared and hated by the Jews. James E. Talmage provides us with some background about him.

> Herod was professedly an adherent of the religion of Judah, though by birth an Idumean, by descent an Edomite or one of the posterity of Esau, all of whom the Jews hated; and of all Edomites not one was more bitterly detested than was Herod the king. He was tyrannical and merciless, sparing neither foe nor friend who came under suspicion of being a possible hindrance to his ambitious designs. He had his wife and several of his sons, as well as others of his blood kindred, cruelly murdered; and he put to death nearly all of the great national council, the Sanhedrin. His reign was one of revolting cruelty and unbridled oppression. Only when in danger of inciting a national revolt or in fear of incurring the displeasure of his imperial master, the Roman emperor, did he stay his hand in any undertaking. (*Jesus the Christ*, 97–98)

When the Wise Men arrived in Jerusalem, they went to the palace of the king to seek directions as to the whereabouts of the Christ child in order to visit Him. Herod asked his advisors about the matter and they had no trouble coming up with the answer. The king then called the Wise Men to him, told them Bethlehem was the location of the Child's birth, and slyly asked them to inform him when they found the Holy Child so that he, too, could worship Him.

> When Herod the king had heard these things, he was troubled, and all Jerusalem with him.
> And when he had gathered all the chief priests and scribes of the people together, he demanded of them where Christ should be born.
> And they said unto him, In Bethlehem of Judæa: for thus it is written by the prophet,
> And thou Bethlehem, in the land of Juda, art not the least among the princes of Juda: for out of thee shall come a Governor, that shall rule my people Israel.

Then Herod, when he had privily called the wise men, inquired of them diligently what time the star appeared.

And he sent them to Bethlehem, and said, Go and search diligently for the young child; and when ye have found him, bring me word again, that I may come and worship him also. (Matthew 2:3–8)

The JST makes changes in verses 4–6, above.

JST Matthew 2:4–6

And when he had gathered all the chief priests, and scribes of the people together, he demanded of them, *saying, Where is the place that is written of by the prophets, in which* Christ should be born? *For he greatly feared, yet he believed not the prophets.*

And they said unto him, It is written by the prophets, that he should be born in Bethlehem of Judea, *for thus have they said,*

The word of the Lord came unto us, saying, And thou Bethlehem, *which lieth* in the land of Judea, *in thee shall be born a prince, which* art not the least among the princes of Judea; for out of thee shall come the Messiah, who shall save my people Israel.

The Wise Men were guided by a star to the house in which Joseph, Mary, and the young Child were staying. Overjoyed when they arrived, these righteous men from the East then worshipped Him, presenting Him gifts of gold, frankincense, and myrrh. Perhaps it is the fact that Matthew mentions three specific gifts that gives rise to the often repeated but unsubstantiated notion that there were three of them. Gold was, of course, a very valuable gift. Frankincense and myrrh were likewise costly gifts, highly prized for their use as pleasant-smelling incense in this culture where sanitation was a concern and incense helped mask unpleasant odors. Also, it may well be that these gifts from the Wise Men helped pay expenses for the trip to Egypt, mentioned in Matthew 2:13.

When they had heard the king, they departed; and, lo, the star, which they saw in the east, went before them, till it came and stood over where the young child was.

When they saw the star, they rejoiced with exceeding great joy.

And when they were come into the house, they saw the young child with Mary his mother, and fell down, and worshipped him: and when they had opened their treasures, they presented unto him gifts; gold, and frankincense, and myrrh. (Matthew 2:9–11)

After visiting and worshipping the Child, these humble men were warned by God not to go back to Herod as he had requested and report of their visit to the Christ child and His current location. Rather, they were instructed to leave the area by another route.

And being warned of God in a dream that they should not return to Herod, they departed into their own country another way. (Matthew 2:12)

Herod Orders the Slaughter of Children in and around Bethlehem

King Herod was furious when he discovered that the Wise Men had disobeyed his request to report back to him. As a result, he ordered the slaughter of all children (in the Greek Bible, it says "male children") two years old and under in Bethlehem and the surrounding regions. According to his calculations, based on what he had learned from the Wise Men, that action should eliminate the Christ child and any threat to Herod's position as king from this supposed "King of the Jews" (Matthew 2:2).

Then Herod, when he saw that he was mocked of the wise men, was exceeding wroth, and sent forth, and slew all the children

[Greek: male children] that were in Bethlehem, and in all the coasts thereof, from two years old and under, according to the time which he had diligently inquired of the wise men. (Matthew 2:16)

Zacharias Is Slain for Refusing to Disclose Young John the Baptist's Whereabouts

At this time, John the Baptist was also a young child, just six months older than Jesus (Luke 1:36), and his parents were apparently living in the Bethlehem area. Joseph Smith informs us that John's father, Zacharias, was murdered by the soldiers of King Herod for refusing to disclose the whereabouts of young John.

When Herod's edict went forth to destroy the young children, John was about six months older than Jesus, and came under this hellish edict, and Zacharias caused his mother to take him into the mountains, where he was raised on locusts and wild honey. When his father refused to disclose his hiding place, and being the officiating high priest at the Temple that year, was slain by Herod's order, between the porch and the altar. (*Teachings of the Prophet Joseph Smith*, 261)

During the last week of His mortal mission, Jesus alluded to the murder of righteous Zacharias as He scolded the scribes and Pharisees for being hypocrites and persecuting and killing the prophets He had sent to them.

Wherefore, behold, I send unto you prophets, and wise men, and scribes: and some of them ye shall kill and crucify; and some of them shall ye scourge in your synagogues, and persecute them from city to city:

That upon you may come all the righteous blood shed upon the earth, from the blood of righteous Abel unto the blood of Zacharias son of Barachias, whom ye slew between the temple and the altar. (Matthew 23:34–35)

Joseph Follows the Lord's Commands

After the Wise Men left, Joseph was told by an angel in a dream to take Jesus and His mother and flee to Egypt, where they would be out of Herod's reach and where they were to remain until he received further word from God. Joseph did not delay and the small family fled by night and traveled to Egypt (Matthew 2:13–15). Matthew's account tells us that they remained in Egypt until Joseph was told by an angel in a dream that Herod had died and it was now safe to take his family back to the land of Israel (Matthew 2:19–20). Upon returning, Joseph found out that Herod's son, Archelaus, was ruling in his place. Consequently, Joseph took his little family to Galilee and settled in Nazareth, rather than remaining in Judea (Matthew 2:21–23). Have you noticed what a good man Joseph was? He had the gift of "beholding of angels" (Moroni 10:14) through which he received messages from God. He was blessed with communication from God in dreams. And he was faithful and obedient to what he was told in these revelations and likely in all others God sent him.

The Only Begotten of the Father in the Flesh

In fulfillment of numerous prophecies given of His birth by ancient prophets from the beginning—including one as recent as five years before the event, given by Samuel the Lamanite (Helaman 14:2)—the "Only Begotten of the Father in the Flesh" had now entered mortality with Mary as His mother and Joseph as his noble stepfather. He was the Son of God. As a result of His parentage, He had divine power over death and also the ability to experience mortality and die. A beautiful summary of these attributes of the Savior was given to King Benjamin by an angel. Subsequently, he quoted the angel's testimony to his people during his farewell address to them.

> For behold, the time cometh, and is not far distant, that with power, the Lord Omnipotent who reigneth, who was, and is from all eternity to all eternity, shall come down from heaven among the children of men, and shall dwell in a tabernacle of clay, and shall go forth amongst men, working mighty miracles, such as healing the sick, raising the dead, causing the lame to walk, the blind to receive their sight, and the deaf to hear, and curing all manner of diseases.
>
> And he shall cast out devils, or the evil spirits which dwell in the hearts of the children of men.
>
> And lo, he shall suffer temptations, and pain of body, hunger, thirst, and fatigue, even more than man can suffer, except it be unto death; for behold, blood cometh from every pore, so great shall be his anguish for the wickedness and the abominations of his people.
>
> And he shall be called Jesus Christ, the Son of God, the Father of heaven and earth, the Creator of all things from the beginning; and his mother shall be called Mary. (Mosiah 3:5–8)

In Conclusion

The Virgin Mary was made aware early on that her name would be well known. She declared prophetically that "from henceforth all generations shall call me blessed" (Luke 1:48). Doctrine & Covenants 76:24 expands our vision as to the extent that this inspired utterance has been and will be fulfilled. It teaches us that our Savior is also the Savior of all Heavenly Father's worlds. In Moses 1:33, we are informed that the Father already has "worlds without number." We know also that He is an exalted being and will yet continue having more spirit children, having "a continuation of the seeds forever and ever" (D&C 132:19), and sending them in their turn to an infinite number of worlds He has created and those yet to be created. With these revealed facts in mind, we picture that Mary is well known not only upon our earth but also upon worlds without number, as prophets there also teach and preach about the Savior's virgin birth and mortal mission to atone and redeem, carried out on our world.

As with all things vast and beyond mortal comprehension, satisfaction for the soul still resides in the simplest of human feelings combined with the pure witness and instruction from the Spirit. As we stretch our minds to appreciate the wonder and vastness of the Savior's atoning mission to cleanse and heal, we find our deepest satisfaction and security in the simple witness of the Spirit that Mary's Son is indeed our Savior and Redeemer. Our gratitude to Him and to our Father is eternal. Our appreciation for Mary is pure and powerfully simple as the Spirit bears witness to our souls that the virgin birth was indeed exactly that. Through the power of the Holy Ghost, we know and deeply feel the warmth of bright hope associated with living the gospel now and anticipating eternal life in the presence of the Father and the Son, along with our families and loved ones, forever. No doubt we will, through our faithfulness, be privileged in a future time to embrace Mary and express in person our admiration and reverence for her. In the meantime, each Christmas season brings renewed appreciation for her and heightens our gratitude for her sacrifices to bring forth the Son of God for His mortal mission.

About the Author

David J. Ridges taught for the Church Educational System for thirty-five years and taught for several years at BYU Campus Education Week. He taught adult religion classes and Know Your Religion classes for BYU Continuing Education for many years. He has also served as a curriculum writer for Sunday School, seminary, and institute of religion manuals.

He has served in many callings in the Church, including Gospel Doctrine teacher, bishop, stake president, and patriarch.

He and Sister Ridges have served two full-time CES missions together. They are the parents of six children and grandparents of eleven grandchildren so far. They make their home in Springville, Utah.